7194   20p

CW01521626

Lightning Lucy Strikes Again

Jeremy Strong

Illustrated by Toni Goffe

A&C Black · London

The Crackers Series

Strong, Jeremy
  Lightning Lucy strikes again.
  —(The Crackers series)
  I. Title   II. Series
  823'.914[J]   PZ7

  ISBN 0-7136-2647-X

Published by A & C Black (Publishers) Limited
35 Bedford Row, London WC1R 4JH

The illustrations are by Toni Goffe

ISBN 0-7136-2647-X

Filmset by August Filmsetting, Haydock, St Helens
Printed in Great Britain by Biddles Ltd, Guildford, Surrey

Identified Flying Objects

When Lucy King was just six months old her pram was struck by lightning. As she was fast asleep inside at the time, her parents were terribly worried. They rushed out to her and were astonished to discover that she was quite unharmed. In fact, she was lying in her pram and gurgling with laughter, whilst the pram itself had a faint red glow all around it, from the huge shock of electricity that had passed through it.

Of course Mr and Mrs King thought their daughter had had a miraculous escape and eventually they almost forgot about it. But as she grew up Lucy began to behave rather oddly.

When she was four she fell into the goldfish pond. Before her startled parents could rush to her aid, Lucy had zoomed out of the pond and flown – flown! – up to the safety of the apple tree.

At the age of seven she rescued her younger brother, Nicholas, from certain death. A truck was about to run him over. Lucy flew across the road and swept him up out of harm's way.

Mr and Mrs King had to accept that their daughter could fly. Then Lucy discovered that if she thought hard enough about an object she could make *that* fly too. So she thought very hard about Nicholas and made him fly through the air and then land upside down on top of her wardrobe. Neither Mum nor Nicholas had been very pleased about that, but Lucy was delighted.

The trouble was that Lucy was a bit of a scatterbrain and although she seemed to have the most marvellous powers they got her into as many awkward spots as good ones. However, one stormy afternoon she had managed to stop a whole herd of cows stampeding through the town centre, whilst amazed shoppers watched. It was then that she became known as 'Lightning Lucy'.

A grateful shop owner even offered the Kings a free holiday in Greece as a reward for saving his shop from being wrecked by rampaging cows. The Kings were not very rich and it was a marvellous opportunity. So, thanks to Lucy, the whole family went off to Greece for four weeks.

They had a wonderful time. They swam and sunbathed and saw all the sights. They danced themselves silly at the discos and ate strange food. Nicholas found a baby octopus when he went diving and wanted to bring it home, but Mum wouldn't let him. The only time Lucy had to use her special power was when Nicholas fell over the balcony rail. She whizzed down in a shower of sparks and grabbed him before he hit the ground. She was getting used to that sort of thing.

Now it was their last day in Greece, and Lucy was gazing fondly round the little bedroom that had been home for the last four weeks.

'I don't want to go home,' she murmured. 'I shall have to start piano practice again.'

'And we shall have to go back to school,' said Nicholas. 'Why don't we stay behind?'

'How can we do that?'

'Easy. We could hide inside a cupboard or something.'

'Don't be daft,' said Lucy. 'Mum and Dad would look for you. They'd soon find you.'

'I'll hide somewhere they can't find me,' insisted Nicholas.

'They won't go without you.'

Nicholas grinned. 'In that case we shall all have to stay behind!' He crumpled up his last pair of shorts, rammed them into his suitcase and sat on the lid.

Lucy went to the balcony and stared out across the blue sea. She sighed.

'Come on. Let's go downstairs. Mum and Dad will be waiting at our table. They said it will be special tonight because it's our last proper meal in Greece.'

'Race you!' yelled Nicholas, hastily adding, 'and you're not allowed to fly. That's cheating.' He skidded out of the room and went pounding downstairs two at a time. Lucy was right behind him. Together they burst into the dining room and thundered across to their table.

'Please, please!' cried Mrs King. 'Don't come into the dining room like that.'

'We were having a race,' panted Nicholas. 'I won.'

'No you didn't!' shouted Lucy. 'I sat down before you.'

'But I got to the dining room before you,' cried Nicholas.

'And I shall send you both back upstairs if you can't behave properly,' interrupted Dad. He glared at them for a few moments, daring them to speak. Then he smiled. 'Well, our last meal. Why don't we have a bottle of champagne, to celebrate our holiday?'

'Champagne!' Lucy cried.

'Fantastic!' said Nicholas, his eyes as big as wine glasses.

Mrs King touched her husband's arm gently. 'Are you sure we can afford it, dear?' He grinned at her and winked.

'It's not proper French champagne. It's just fizzy wine really, but I don't suppose we shall notice the difference. We don't get much practice at sipping champagne, do we?'

Mrs King was still looking a little concerned. 'What about the children? Do you think it's all right for them?'

'Of course it is. One glass won't do them any harm.' Mr King nudged his wife. 'It's me you've got to worry about. Too much champagne and I go all bubbly myself!'

Mrs King laughed. 'The sooner we all get home, the better. Maybe things will be normal then, though how anything can ever be normal with Lucy around, I don't know. Ah! Here comes the waiter.'

It wasn't long before they were all eating away at platefuls of food. The bottle of champagne arrived, nestling in a big bucket of ice. Lucy and Nicholas were delighted when the waiter popped the cork so that it flew across the room, bounced off the ceiling and almost ended up in somebody's soup.

The waiter poured out four glasses of champagne. Then the bubbles in the drink got up Nicholas's nose and he sneezed. Everybody in the dining room turned to see what was going on.

'That sneeze sounded like another cork going off,' said Lucy with a little giggle.

'I don't think it was that funny,' said Mum, but the bubbles began to work on her and she started smiling too.

After twenty minutes all the Kings were getting giggly. Lucy finished her glass of champagne and Mr King poured out a second glass for her.

'Do you think that's wise, Harold?' Mrs King asked her husband.

'It is our last day,' Mr King pointed out. Lucy's eyes popped with delight and she took a huge sip.

The waiter came and cleared their plates. He took their orders for pudding. Nicholas watched him hurry back to the kitchen.

'I'm glad I'm not a waiter,' he said. 'They have to do so much rushing backwards and forwards. Kitchen to table to kitchen to table . . . I'm glad I'm not one.'

'What – a table?' asked Lucy.

'No, you stupid dustbrain!'

'Well, are you glad you're not a kitchen then?'

'No!'

'That's what you said. You said that you were glad you weren't . . .'

'All right Lucy,' Dad interrupted. 'That's enough.'

Lucy grinned at Nicholas and whispered to him. 'I know what I'd do if I were a waiter. I wouldn't keep rushing around like a mad penguin.'

'What would you do?' asked Nicholas.

'I'd make all the tables come to me. I'd make them rise up in the air and come to me.'

'You couldn't do that, could you?'

'Of course I could.' Lucy began to giggle once more. 'It would be easy.' She watched a waiter hurry to a table and then back to the kitchen. Another waiter burst out from the kitchen, with trays of food in both hands.

There was a startled cry from the far end of the dining room. A chair toppled over, throwing a fat old holiday-maker to the floor. Everybody stared across at the far corner. One of the huge round dining tables was rising up in the air. It hovered overhead and slowly began to revolve. Then it skimmed across the room with its tablecloth gently flapping, just below the ceiling. The waiter went plunging after it with his plates of food.

Nicholas was falling off his chair with the giggles. 'It's an unidentified flying table!' he crowed. Lucy sat very quietly with a faint red glow all around her and a distant look in her twinkling eyes. Mum and Dad guessed exactly what was going on.

'Lucy!' hissed Dad. 'Lucy stop it! Put that table down at once!'

But Lucy was in a trance of concentration and the table went on travelling round the room, with the waiter stumbling after it, puffing and panting and desperate to put his hot plates down.

Mum leant across the table and seized Lucy by the arm.

'Stop it, Lucy!' Mum shook her daughter violently. The floating table lurched sideways and everything slid off and rained down on the tables beneath; plates, cups, food, glasses, knives, forks – everything. Then the table went into a nose-dive and crashed to the floor where it lay on one side, rolling drunkenly.

'Oh Lucy!' wailed Mum. Lucy shook out her crackling curls and started giggling.

'It wasn't my fault. If you hadn't disturbed me it would have landed perfectly.'

'I doubt it,' said Dad. 'Anyway, it's certainly nothing to laugh about.' He watched the waiters clearing up the mess. The dining room was buzzing with excited chatter as the diners wondered how it had all happened. It was an amazing mystery, except to the Kings.

Nicholas began laughing again, and that made Lucy start up.

'Unidentified flying tables!' he spluttered again.

'Intergalactic soup-bowls!' hooted Lucy.

Mr and Mrs King stood up. They glanced at each other and nodded. 'I think it might be a good idea to get these two up to bed,' said Mum. 'Something tells me they've had a little bit too much to drink.' She sighed. 'The sooner we get back home, the better.'

But even as she said it she knew that no matter where they were, Lucy would always be Lightning Lucy and there would be storms wherever she went.

2

Lost Luggage

The first thing that happened to the Kings when they arrived at the airport back in England was that their luggage got lost. They searched and searched, but couldn't see it anywhere.

'It's like looking for a needle in a haystack,' grumbled Mr King, as he stared around at the great mounds of cases and bags and trunks and rucksacks that kept on being unloaded from the arriving planes.

'Are you sure you labelled them properly?' asked Mrs King.

'Of course I did!' snapped Dad.

'Maybe they've been sent to another country,' Lucy suggested.

'And we shall have to go there to get them back,' added Nicholas, with a sly smile.

Mr King paced angrily up and down. 'There must be thousands of cases here,' he declared. 'It's no good – I shall have to go and search the whole airport. You stay here and keep an eye on this moving luggage belt, just in case it comes through that way. I'll have a look round and see if I can get anybody to help.'

He strode off and soon vanished among the crowds of people who were bustling about, pushing and shoving and shouting at each other in twenty different languages.

Nicholas climbed up the barrier that separated them from the moving luggage belt, and sat astride it. It was fascinating watching the luggage come through: tartan bags, brown bags, blue bags, leather suitcases and strangely shaped packages – all too big to go in the luggage racks of the plane.

Mrs King kept standing on tiptoe, to see over the heads of the seething crowd. She was hoping to spot her husband. She glanced anxiously at her watch as time went by and told Lucy she was afraid Dad had got himself lost.

'I'll go and look for him,' offered Lucy, but Mum grabbed her by the collar before Lucy could disappear into the crowd as well.

'You stay here,' said Mum. 'I don't want both of you lost. We shall do far better waiting together.'

Lucy joined Nicholas at the barrier. He pointed to the end of the luggage belt, rumbling away on the other side.

'Look,' he said, 'you can see where all the cases get sorted into a single line. Then that machine at the side weighs each case and the big blue thing above comes down and stamps a label on it and it disappears down that little tunnel. I suppose it goes to the plane after that.'

Lucy watched all the luggage being sorted, weighed and stamped. It was almost hypnotic. She saw the baggage vanish down the tunnel, and an odd thought came to her.

'Nicholas,' she said, 'if all that luggage is being stamped to go on the aeroplanes, why are we waiting here to try and find ours? Our luggage should be coming off the plane, not going onto it.'

Nicholas's jaw dropped open and he gazed at his sister for several seconds. 'You'd better tell Mum,' he whispered. Lucy told Mum and Mum smiled and told them not to be silly. Dad knew what he was doing.

'He can't possibly have made us wait all this time in the wrong place,' she said. 'Just keep an eye on that luggage belt.' Then she had a quick glance round to see if there were any signs to show that they were waiting in the wrong place.

Suddenly several things happened at once. Mr King came hurrying out of the crowd, shouting and waving. At the same time a huge, fat old gentleman bustled up against Nicholas and knocked him from his perch on the barrier. He landed head first amongst the moving suitcases and bags. For a moment he was dazed. Then he struggled to the surface and shouted.

'Help!'

The Kings turned to stare. They were just in time to see Nicholas being weighed. Then he was under the blue machine and a label was being stuck on top of his head.

'Do something, Harold!' wailed Mrs King.

'Stop the luggage belt!' yelled Mr King.

'Ouch!' cried Nicholas, trying to peel the label off his head, whilst the tunnel that led to the departing planes came closer and closer, a huge black mouth ready to gobble Nicholas up and make him disappear forever, probably to Peru or Tibet or somewhere like that.

Suddenly, there was a fizz of sparks and Lucy leaped into action. Down she darted at lightning speed, grabbed her brother's arm and pulled him from the mouth of the tunnel. She sped back to Mum and Dad and plonked Nicholas down beside them. Then she shook her mass of fair curls and tiny red sparks glittered as they fell to the floor.

'Honestly Nicholas,' she complained, 'I'm getting fed up with rescuing you. I wish you'd learn to fly for yourself.'

The other travellers were nudging each other and pointing at Lucy.

'Did you see that? She flew through the air!'

'She saved that little boy's life!'

'. . .just like Superman, and she was glowing all over . . .'

Mr King hustled his family along in front of him. This was the last thing he wanted. He hated it when everybody saw Lucy's amazing powers. He knew it wasn't her fault, and her powers were often very useful, but he didn't like all the attention it brought them. They had gone away on holiday to escape all the attention. Now, the moment they were back in England Lucy was zooming around and they were the centre of attraction once again.

'Come on,' he muttered. 'Keep moving. Let's get out of here before somebody starts asking questions and they find out who you are. They'll only want photographs and autographs and everything.'

'What about the luggage?' asked Mrs King.

'I've found that. You were waiting in the wrong place. That was where the luggage was being put on the plane.'

'See? I told you, Mum,' said Lucy.

'And I told you,' butted in Nicholas. 'I noticed it first.'

'You didn't! All you said was . . .'

'I did, I did! You always pinch my ideas. Just because you can fly you think you're brilliant but . . .'

'Shut up!' yelled Dad. The whole airport froze and turned to stare at Mr King, rapidly turning a very embarassed purple colour. 'Will you two stop quarrelling for one minute?' he hissed. 'Here's the luggage. Everybody take a case each and if you two say another word again I'll, I'll, I'll, . . . put Nicholas and Lucy back on the luggage belt. Then maybe we'll get a bit of peace!'

They managed to get outside the airport without any more wars. Mr King called a taxi and it wasn't very long before they were pulling up outside their own home.

They hardly recognised it. The house was covered in coloured streamers and little flags.

There was a sheet hanging from two upstairs windows, with large red letters sprawled across it.

WELCOME HOME LIGHTNING LUCY
OUR HEROINE!!

Lucy jumped out of the taxi and stared. 'Wow!' she breathed. Nicholas slumped back in his seat and muttered something about his sister's head getting too big for her to get through their front door any longer.

'Come on,' coaxed Mum. 'Give us a hand with the luggage. Lucy can't help being special you know. We're really quite lucky to have such a clever girl in the family.' Then Mum bent down close and whispered into Nicholas's left ear. 'Only don't ever tell Lucy that, or she *will* get big-headed!' Nicholas laughed and grabbed one of the cases.

The neighbours were very kind. They had prepared a special tea for all the family, and the Kings felt rather proud and a bit embarassed.

'You shouldn't have gone to all this trouble,' murmured Mrs King.

'Nonsense,' cried Mr Jackson from across the road. 'It's not every street that has a real super-hero – I mean, super-heroine – living in it. We're all jolly pleased. I always thought Lucy was a lovely girl.'

Lucy overheard this last remark and wondered why Mr Jackson had been so rude to her a couple of months earlier if he thought she was a lovely girl.

After all, it wasn't her fault that his dog had been so scared by her zooming across the park that it had jumped into the duck pond.

Mr and Mrs King were very pleased when the tea party was over and everybody was able to go back to their homes. They took down the bunting and the sheet hanging out of the upstairs windows. Then they set about putting things straight after their four week holiday.

They unpacked the suitcases and sorted out the dirty washing and put all their souvenirs out on display. Nicholas seemed to have brought back nothing but bits of rock.

'What do you want those for?' demanded Lucy.

'When I have a bath I'm going to stick them in the middle, and then I shall have my own Greek island,' he explained.

'Call the doctor, Mum,' sighed Lucy. 'Nick's gone potty.'

Mum wagged a finger at Lucy. 'Don't call him Nick. It sounds terrible. He's got a proper name, so use it.'

Nicholas looked up from arranging his rocks. 'I don't mind being called Nick. I like it.'

'Don't argue,' snapped Mum. Nicholas glanced at Lucy and shrugged.

Mrs King made a cup of tea while Mr King made sure the children had a good bath before he settled them in bed. At length he came downstairs quietly and flopped into an armchair. Mrs King passed him his tea.

'There are three sacks of letters waiting for Lucy to open,' she said. Mr King groaned.

'Oh no, I thought we might have said goodbye to all that. I was hoping people would have forgotten about her by now. Will we never get any peace? Why can't we just live ordinary lives, like everybody else? It can't go on. It will drive us mad.'

Mrs King nodded. 'What can we do?' she asked.

Mr King rubbed his forehead and took several sips from his tea. At length he looked up at his wife. 'We could always go and live somewhere else,' he said. 'Yes – we could move house.'

3

The Football Tournament

Lucy was not very fond of school. Her teacher, Mr Barber, was all right. He was quite kind really, and only shouted at her about five times every day. Lucy thought this wasn't too bad because her friend Robert got shouted at about twenty times a day.

The problem was that Lucy didn't like work at all, and just recently she had begun to spend all her time thinking about soccer and nothing else. It was her latest passion.

Robert was in the school team and Lucy played soccer with him and his friends every playtime. They all thought she was pretty good. When she got home, Lucy would pester Mrs King to fit her out with the colours of her favourite team, but since Lucy changed her favourite team every week Mrs King decided it wasn't worth it.

One morning at assembly, Mrs Conway, the head teacher, told the school that there was going to be a football tournament for the local schools. Their school would take part, as usual. They had won the tournament for the last two years, and if they won it again this year it would be a hat-trick and they would be allowed to keep the big silver trophy for ever. Usually the trophy was kept by the winners just for the year and then handed over to the new winners.

Mrs Conway pointed out that the school team had been playing very well this season and had won most of their matches.

'However,' she continued, 'we must not get big-headed about it. There are one or two tough teams that we shall have to beat. Downsland School will be taking part and I hear that their team is very strong this year. Well, the tournament takes place this week-end, so let's wish our team the best of luck.'

After assembly, Lucy spoke to Robert.

'I wish I was playing. Are you going to be in the team, Robert?'

'Probably. I don't fancy playing the Downsland team though.'

'Are they really good?'

Robert gave a hollow laugh. 'They're no good at all. They foul all the time. They trip you up and kick and push, but somehow the ref never notices. I bet you we have to play them in the final—if we make it that far!'

Lucy clapped him on the shoulders. 'Of course you'll make it to the final! You're brilliant!'

'I wish you were playing for us,' said Robert. Lucy's face went glum all over.

'Fat chance,' she muttered.

Then awful things began to happen to the football team. The right-wing got chicken pox. Their star goal scorer tripped over his new puppy at home and fell and broke his arm. To make matters worse even the school's amazing goalkeeper (nicknamed 'Octopus' because his hands were all over the goal mouth) knocked himself out on a goal post during training. He was carried off to hospital and was told to stay there for two days. That meant he would miss the tournament.

Mr Barber, who looked after the football team, was going frantic. He had already used his reserves filling the first two places. He searched all the classes for signs of a good new goalkeeper, but there was no-one.

The day before the tournament Mr Barber sat moodily at his desk, wondering what to do. Robert took up his work book to be checked. Mr Barber was so deep in thought he didn't even notice.

Robert waited and eventually coughed loudly. Mr Barber gave a startled jump, but instead of being cross he mumbled an apology.

'Sorry, Robert. I was just trying to figure out what to do with the football team tomorrow. Three of our best players won't be there and I can't find anybody to replace Octopus. I'm afraid we're going to lose that cup.' Mr Barber heaved a sigh and continued to stare blankly into space.

Robert nodded slowly. 'Why don't you try Lucy King, Mr Barber? She often plays with us at playtime and she's ex.'

'Ex?' repeated Mr Barber. 'What's ex?'

'Ex! You know – excellent, ace, brill!'

Mr Barber frowned and looked across at Lucy. She was leaning far back on her chair, as usual, and talking noisily to the girl behind her. He could see she hadn't done a stroke of work all morning. He groaned to himself.

'She *is* good Mr Barber,' said Robert once more. Mr Barber nodded reluctantly. He didn't have much choice.

'All right, I'll have a word with her. Lucy!' There was a loud clatter as Lucy fell off her chair in guilty surprise. The class began to laugh and Lucy clambered out from the wreckage.

'All right, class,' said Mr Barber. 'Get on with your work. Lucy, I want a word with you.'

When Lucy discovered that Mr Barber wanted to try her out as goalkeeper in the team she was over the moon. She went home walking on air, which made a change from flying through it. She was so excited that she dreamed all night about scoring six million goals, all with her left foot.

At the weekend the whole family turned up for the football tournament. There were about ten schools taking part. The first three matches were fairly easy and Lucy had little work to do. She only let in one goal and the rest of the team played well and scored quite a few. They got through to the semi-final.

'Do your best,' Mr Barber told them, quite unecessarily. 'Downsland are playing in the other semi-final. Let's hope they don't make it.'

The semi-final was a tough match. The other team were good and Lucy let in three goals. This upset her and she felt useless.

'Don't give up,' shouted Robert, racing upfield after the ball.

'But I've let in three,' Lucy wailed.

'And you've saved hundreds!' he pointed out.

In the end Lucy's school won 5–4. It had been too close for Lucy's liking. To make matters worse, Downsland won their match 9–1. It was a taste of things to come. Lucy felt like giving up on the spot.

The rest of the team were pretty downcast too. Some of them had played Downsland before.

They had a half-hour break before the final to get their strength back. Then it was back onto the pitch.

Mr and Mrs King and Nicholas stood on the touchline, cheering their heads off. The referee blew the whistle and the match started. Downsland were onto the ball straightaway. Their star player was about two metres tall and built like a gorilla – or so he seemed to Lucy as he charged towards her with the ball at his feet. He slammed it straight at her and she had the breath knocked clean from her body in saving it.

'Well done Lucy!' yelled Mr King. The Downsland Gorilla stood over her.

'Lucy?' he snarled. 'Lucy?' He turned upfield and bellowed.

'Hey – their goalie's a girl! She's a girl!' He ran upfield punching his fist in the air and yelling, 'We'll massacre them! Girlies! Girlies!'

Lucy got her breath back and kicked the ball upfield. Her eyes blazed. If only she could use her power to lift that great stinking gorilla into the air and drop him off somewhere nice, like the nearby duck-pond. Her hair crackled with electricity and she stretched out her fingers. There was a sharp voice behind her.

'Don't do it,' warned Mr Barber, who knew all about Lucy's special tricks. 'You'll get the whole team disqualified.'

Lucy lowered her arms helplessly. She watched the tussle for the ball going on, then Downsland came thundering back. The defence went sprawling in the mud. They couldn't get near the ball. The Downsland gorilla loomed into view and pounded the ball into the net.

After that it went on and on. Downsland kept coming back and every time Lucy's team tried to tackle they ended up crashing to the ground. Soon two of the team had been taken off with twisted ankles and bruised shins and there was nobody to replace them. They complained about the fouling but the ref seemed to be deaf – not to mention blind.

Poor Lucy couldn't keep up with the relentless attack. Downsland would come right up to the goal mouth before they even took a kick. They could hardly miss. When the first half finished the score was 7–2 to Downsland, and Lucy's team only had eight players left.

Mr and Mrs King tried to cheer the team up, especially Lucy, who felt she was letting her side down dreadfully. Nicholas wanted Lucy to make the whole Downsland team float away to the top of Mount Everest but Mr King said why spoil Mount Everest? It hadn't done any harm.

That cheered the team up a little and they went back onto the pitch determined to do their best. But Lucy was still thoroughly fed up. It just wasn't a fair match. She really wanted to use her powers but she knew that if anybody saw, then the team would be disqualified. It was not until the Downsland Gorilla scored an eighth goal and called her 'Girly!' for the hundredth time that she began to have an idea.

The next time she kicked the ball upfield she gave it a little extra help. The ball turned very faintly red and not only travelled twice as far but landed beautifully, right at the feet of their centre half. He leaped on the ball, whisked it forward and scored from a powering long shot.

Lucy did that several more times, until Mr Barber came and stood behind the goal and watched her closely, with a severe frown on his face. Lucy wondered if he wasn't smiling just a little too. Anyhow, he couldn't see what she was doing because she didn't even need to point her fingers as the ball was so light.

Then Downsland got the ball once more and came stampeding back down the pitch. Lucy smiled to herself and waited. The Downsland Gorilla took an almighty swipe at the ball, but somehow the ball wasn't there any longer. It had sort of moved sideways. The Gorilla kicked the empty air and fell flat on his back in the mud. Lucy grabbed the ball, kicked it upfield and placed it just right for a goal.

Now every time Downsland got near Lucy's goal strange things happened. The ball would hop sideways or jump up and bonk the Downsland players on the head. Sometimes a shot would come straight at the goal and stop dead, as if it had hit an invisible force, which of course it had. Lucy leaned against a goal post, with her hair sticking out a bit more than usual.

Gradually the score changed and the Downsland players became more and more furious. When the Gorilla fell over for the sixth time after trying to kick a ball that wasn't there Lucy called out to him.

'Would you like a hand getting up? I'm only a girl, but you seem a little wobbly on your pegs today!'

The Downsland Gorilla struggled up, plucked a huge clod of mud from his hair and hurled it at her. It missed of course.

When the final whistle went, the score was 11–9 to Lucy's team. She was carried shoulder-high round the pitch, while Mr and Mrs King talked quietly with Mr Barber.

'Strange match, wasn't it?' said Mr Barber, with a ghost of a smile. 'Did you see Lucy do anything, because I didn't.'

Mr King grinned. 'I didn't see Lucy do anything, but I saw the ball do the most extraordinary things. Do you know, it almost made me think that ball had special powers!'

All three of them shook their heads and laughed, while the victorious team collected the silver trophy. It was theirs to keep.

4

Lucy Plays with Fire

Being a member of a triumphant football team did a lot for Lucy. She did everything a little better. Her school work was neater and she didn't fall off her chair quite so often.

'It's a miracle,' said Mr Barber. 'Let's just hope it lasts.'

Lucy played for the team regularly and it kept her busy all through the winter. She was quite sorry when the football season ended.

'I wish we could play all year round,' she confided to Robert.

'I'm going to try and get in the cricket team,' Robert said. 'Why don't you?'

'Cricket! What do you want to play that game for? All you do is stand in the middle of a field all day long. You might as well decide to be a cow.'

'Mooo!' teased Robert, and he went off to practice his bowling.

Once more Lucy was left with nothing to do. She began to lose interest in other things and soon her work had slipped back into the untidy mess it had been before.

'I knew it couldn't last,' sighed Mr Barber, all to himself.

One day, when Lucy and Nicholas got home from school, Mrs King had news for them. They had managed to sell the house, and in a couple of months they would be moving.

'But where are we going?' asked Lucy.

'Back to Greece?' suggested Nicholas hopefully.

'I'm afraid Greece will have to wait until we win lots of money,' smiled Mrs King. 'But do you remember that house we went to look at last month – the one with the long garden and the swing? We're going to move there. It's not too far, so you won't have to change school. We simply must get away from here. Every day there seem to be more callers wanting Lucy's autograph or wanting her to do something special for them. Your father and I don't get a moment's peace.'

Lucy and Nicholas looked glum. They didn't want to move at all. They had spent all their lives in the same house. It didn't seem possible to change anything now.

'What about my bedroom and everything?' Lucy asked.

'You'll have a new bedroom. You can choose some wallpaper for it if you like'

Lucy brightened up. 'Can I have that one with the motorbikes roaring across doing wheelies and things?'

Mrs King winced. 'I hardly think that's suitable for your bedroom, Lucy.'

'Oh, Mum!'

'I should think the noise of the bikes would keep you awake all night. Can't you think of something a bit more peaceful?'

Lucy thought. 'There's quite a good one with Indians about to ambush the United States Cavalry, and the captain or general or whatever has got a spear in his back and he's falling off his horse with blood drip . . .'

'Lucy! You are not going to have wallpaper with blood dripping from it. Now please! Let's forget about wallpaper for a moment.'

Lucy wandered aimlessly round the kitchen a few times and then asked what they'd got for tea.

'Liver,' replied Mrs King, and before Lucy could say a thing, she added, 'Don't say a word and don't pull any faces. Liver is very good for you. There's lots of iron in liver.'

'Iron!' cried Lucy. 'I shall go rusty all over. I'll get horrible brown blotches and my arms and legs will fall off!'

Mrs King pointed silently at the kitchen door. She didn't want to hear any more. Lucy grunted and went out. As she reached the door Mrs King called after her.

'You'd better do your piano practice.'

Lucy stopped dead, as if she had just been speared by a wallpaper Indian. 'Oh Mum!'

'Piano practice.'

Lucy stamped off to the front room, trying to make up her mind which was worse – piano practice or liver. She sat down at the keyboard and began to play her scales very slowly.

'Do them properly!' yelled Mum from the kitchen. Lucy played so fast her fingers tripped over each other.

'Do them properly!'

Lucy stopped and thought. There must be something she could do to make piano practice more interesting. She took the piano stool away and tried floating in the air while she thumped out her scales. First she tried floating cross-legged and then she spread out flat, as if she were lying on a bed. It was certainly a lot more fun playing the piano like this. She tried standing upside down, so that her feet were resting on the ceiling.

Nicholas came in and watched her. 'Your face has gone red,' he said. 'All the blood's run to your head. I don't suppose there's any left in your feet. Can I do it too?' Lucy lifted one hand from the piano and pointed at Nicholas. He began to rise slowly from the carpet. Lucy turned him upside down so that they were side by side.

'Do you fancy a walk?' asked Lucy. Nicholas grinned. They held hands and began to walk round the ceiling. 'It's an interesting view, isn't it?' said Lucy, as they hovered over the settee.

The door opened and Mum came in. 'Come down at once! I wondered how those muddy footprints got on your bedroom ceiling Lucy. When are you going to learn that you are not in a circus. Oh! I wish we'd never left you out in that storm.'

Lucy and Nicholas fell in a heap on the settee.

'Now come and have tea. Wash your hands first.'

While they washed their hands, Nicholas and Lucy argued about how much they hated liver.

'I bet I hate it more than you do,' said Nicholas.

'You don't. I hate it so much I'd rather die than eat it.'

'Well I hate it so much I'd rather die twice.'

'Don't be stupid!' snapped Lucy. 'How can you die twice?'

They both snatched at the towel to dry their hands. 'If you get shot with two bullets you die twice,' Nicholas claimed.

'Oh you are so stupid sometimes. You . . .'

'Teatime!' called Mrs King. 'Haven't you two finished yet?'

When they sat down at table Mum was still busy frying the liver. Lucy wrinkled up her nose in disgust. It was one smell she couldn't stand. She glared at the frying pan and wished it would vanish in flames.

'Don't pull faces,' warned Mum. Lucy scowled and glared even harder at the frying pan. The centres of her eyes took on a strange, flickering glow.

Suddenly there was a tremendous bang. The oven door flew off and black smoke billowed from the frying pan. Flames scuttled across the top of the cooker. Mrs King leaped backwards with a strangled cry, dropping the pan and spilling liver across the floor.

Nicholas started yelling, while Lucy simply stared with horror at the flaming gas cooker, her face as white as a ghost.

Mum seized a pan of water and flung it over the cooker. It sizzled and spat and the kitchen was filled with hot steam that smelled even worse than the liver, but the flames went out. Mum wiped her forehead with a sooty tea-towel and opened the door to let out the fumes.

Then she realised someone was crying. It was Lucy. Mrs King hurried over to her daughter.

'Lucy! Whatever is the matter? You haven't been burned, have you?'

Lucy could only shake her head and sob for a long time, but at last she huddled up against Mum and began telling her how she had wished the frying pan would go up in flames and she got this weird feeling of power and suddenly everything seemed to explode and the cooker was in flames and Nicholas was yelling and there was smoke everywhere – it was like a nightmare.

Mum's jaw dropped. 'You mean . . , you mean *you* made it all happen?' she asked incredulously.

Lucy nodded and burst into tears all over again. 'But I didn't mean it to. I didn't know it would happen Mum, honestly I didn't. This strange feeling crept over me. It was horrible.'

Mrs King hugged Lucy tight. 'Don't worry. I'm sure you didn't mean to. Go and play upstairs quietly while I sort things out down here.' Lucy sniffed and went upstairs with Nicholas.

By this time the family cat, Flop, had sneaked in and run off with the burnt liver, so once Mum had cleared the kitchen she had to do a bread and butter tea. That was much more to Lucy's liking.

When Dad came in from work it took a lot of talking to explain why the cooker was black all over and the oven door only hanging on by one hinge. Lucy still looked pale and worried after her new burst of power, and she went up to bed early, leaving Mr and Mrs King to talk things over.

'She worries me,' said Mrs King. 'Is there no end to her powers? Whatever will she do next?'

'I don't like to think,' Mr King answered. 'What concerns me is how we are going to pay for a new cooker. The car practically fell to bits on the way home tonight, so that's going to need paying for. I've no idea where the money is going to come from – not when we are in the middle of all the expense of moving house as well.'

Mr King frowned for a long time. Then he looked up at his wife and smiled. 'I don't suppose Lucy might develop a power for making money?'

Mrs King laughed. 'Knowing our daughter, she would probably make it all in the wrong currency. But it does worry me, this new power. It seems to be uncontrollable.'

'Yes,' mused her husband. 'Rather like Lucy herself – uncontrollable!'

5

Whoops!

Mrs King finished reading her magazine and glanced across at her husband. He was lying on the settee with his eyes closed.

'Are you asleep?' she murmured.

He carefully opened one eye. 'Yes,' he said, 'and I'm dreaming about winning thousands of pounds so that we can buy a new cooker and car,' He sat up and looked searchingly at his wife.

'There's something on your mind,' Mr King said, 'I can tell.'

'It's Lucy. She worries me. I've got used to her being able to fly and make things move about without touching them. But this new power – making things explode into flames – it's so destructive.'

'I know,' sighed Mr King. 'I've seen the cooker – or what's left of it.'

'Lucy's other powers don't do much harm,' Mrs King went on, 'but starting fires is terribly dangerous. Suppose she has a nightmare and uses her new power in her sleep? Her whole bed might go up in flames!'

Mr King got up and put an arm round his wife. 'I'm sure she'll be all right. Let's see how things go.

She's never dreamed about flying, has she? I know she's scatterbrained at times but she's a sensible girl underneath. Besides, she'll be nine shortly.'

'That's another thing,' said Mrs King. 'What are we going to do for her birthday? You know she wants a bike?'

'I don't think we can afford a bike, a new cooker and get the car repaired. Which is most useful?'

'You can't cook on a bicycle,' said Mrs King sharply.

Mr King laughed. 'You can't ride a cooker,' he pointed out. 'I take your point. Moving house is going to be another expense. The bike will have to wait. I know someone at work who's selling a cassette player second-hand. Let's get that.'

Mrs King nodded. 'Okay. We'll have a little party, too.'

Although Mrs King was worried about Lucy's newly discovered power, she wasn't nearly as anxious as Lucy was herself. For days Lucy wandered about hardly daring to look at anything, in case it suddenly burst into flames. She kept her eyes almost shut, and often bumped into things as a result.

More than anything she wanted to find out how her dangerous new power worked. Then maybe she would be able to control it. But finding a chance to try it out wasn't easy.

One afternoon, when nobody was around, she went into the garden and tried staring very hard at things. She didn't have any success, and was just about to go indoors when two of Dad's best cabbages burst into flames, leaving twisted and charred stalks behind.

Lucy hurriedly buried them and hoped Dad would never find out. But she still had no idea why the cabbages had gone up in smoke and nothing else had. It was all very unsettling.

Lucy's birthday came, and luckily it was a Sunday so she didn't have to spend the day at school. Robert came to her party, and so did Paula, another school friend. Robert brought her a Whoopee cushion. Lucy didn't know what to do with it, so Robert blew it up and stuffed it under a cushion on Paula's chair. When Paula sat down it made the most revolting noise and everybody was reduced to hysterical laughter.

Paula had brought Lucy a blank cassette tape. 'It's so that you can record anything,' Paula said. 'Your cassette player's got a microphone, hasn't it? You can record yourself.'

For the next half hour they recorded people sitting on the Whoopee cushion. They recorded Dad leaping into the air and yelling: 'What was that horrible noise!' They taped Mum mumbling: 'Oooh! I do beg your pardon. I must have eaten something that didn't agree with me.'

When tea-time came they all had stomach-ache from laughing so much. Mum brought in a birthday cake she had made herself. The candles were lit, everybody sang 'Happy Birthday to Lucy!' and Lucy made the cake fly round the room before she blew the candles out.

'It was like a space ship,' said Nicholas.

'Like a flying birthday cake,' said Paula, who liked getting things right.

When Paula and Robert were about to leave, Robert whispered in Lucy's ear. 'Are you going to bring the Whoopee cushion to school tomorrow?' Lucy began to giggle. Robert went on. 'You could put it . . . you know!' He started to laugh.

'What are you two whispering about?' asked Mrs King.

'Nothing!' cried Lucy, very guiltily. 'See you tomorrow Robert. 'Bye, Paula.'

'Don't forget!' shouted Robert.

She stood on the steps and waved. Then she went in, collected her presents together and took them upstairs. She was looking forward to tomorrow.

As soon as Lucy got to school she got out the Whoopee cushion and began showing it all round. It caused a great deal of amusement. The only person who didn't find it funny was Maureen Best. Maureen was one of those girls who was brilliant at everything, and that included telling tales. Now Maureen sauntered over and took a cool look at what was going on.

'I think that's silly,' she said. 'It's disgusting.'

'Do you want to sit on it?' offered Lucy.

'Urgh!' winced Maureen, wrinkling up her nose. 'I'd rather sit on a hippo.'

'Poor hippo,' murmured Robert.

When school started Lucy ran into class. Mr Barber hadn't got there yet so she quickly blew up the cushion and shoved it under the cover on his chair. Then she got out her reading book and sat at her desk like an angel. The class settled down.

Mr Barber came in and hung up his jacket. He sorted out some papers on his desk. Lucy held her breath. Mr Barber went to the window and opened it a fraction. He went back to his desk. Then he went to the cupboard, then back to his desk. He stood there a few moments, pulled out his chair and – sat down. PHLLURRRRRPH!!

Mr Barber just sat there until the cushion finished. The class rolled about laughing as if they'd never laughed before. When they stopped Mr Barber slowly got to his feet and pulled the Whoopee cushion out. He held it up.

'I wonder whose this can be?' he asked. There was silence. Then Maureen Best stood up. Mr Barber had never been so surprised.

'Maureen! Is it yours?'

Maureen almost choked and went bright red. 'No, Mr Barber! But I know whose it is. It's Lucy King's.'

Mr Barber sighed. He didn't like people telling tales. All the same, he would have to do something, or the cushion would be turning up in class all day. He looked across at Lucy.

'Is it yours?'

Lucy nodded and waited for the anger to fall on her head, but Mr Barber smiled. 'It's very good,' he said. 'I think it's the best Whoopee cushion I've sat on, but I think we'll put it somewhere safe for the time being. All right?'

Again Lucy nodded and Mr Barber put the cushion away in the cupboard. Lucy heard Maureen sniggering not far to one side of her. She glanced across and saw Maureen put her thumb to her nose, screw up her eyes and waggle her fingers.

Lucy stared back angrily. They'd all been having such good fun with the Whoopee cushion.

She'd been planning to take it out at playtime. Now Maureen Best was grinning madly because she'd spoilt Lucy's fun and had the Whoopee cushion taken away.

Lucy rested her head on one hand and glared across at Maureen. In turn, Maureen poked out her tongue. Lucy's eyes narrowed. A peculiar feeling crept over her, making the hair on the back of her neck prickle. Lucy's eyes began to glow red.

A whisp of smoke trailed out from the lid of Maureen's desk. Maureen sniffed several times and then looked down. The smoke was getting thicker by the second. She gave a squeak of alarm and opened her desk lid. Tongues of flame licked up from her burning books, and a moment later the sides of the desk were alight and smoke was swirling up to the ceiling.

Maureen screamed and toppled backwards off her chair in a dead faint. Mr Barber was already on his feet and yelling, 'Fire! Fire!'

Lucy sat frozen, chilled to the heart by what she had done. The sound of the fire alarm brought her back to life. The room was filling with smoke and Mr Barber was ushering the children to safety. He had Maureen Best slung over one shoulder.

Lucy knew she must act quickly. In a shower of sparks she zoomed into the air and smashed through one of the classroom windows. Like a comet she sped over the school and was soon dragging the hose out of the caretaker's shed.

The playground was full of excited children and teachers, escaping from the spreading flames. They watched in awe as Lucy connected the hose, grabbed the nozzle and went whizzing back to the classroom, with the hose snaking out behind.

There was so much smoke Lucy couldn't see through the broken window. It swirled round her making her choke violently. She pointed the nozzle into the classroom and drenched everything. The burning desk hissed and spluttered and the stench of hot water and ash billowed out, but Lucy stayed there, spraying the classroom until she was quite certain the fire had gone out. She turned off the nozzle and glanced into the dripping, blackened classroom. Lucy had never felt so miserable. Tears began to roll down her cheeks.

Mr Barber came running to her and picked her up. 'Lucy! Thank goodness you're safe. You were incredible! You've saved the school!'

This was too much for Lucy and her shoulders heaved. 'But, but Mr Barber, it was . . . my . . . I . . . I . . .' she stammered, not knowing how to start.

Mrs Conway, the headteacher, came up, looking very concerned.

'Are you all right, Lucy?' she asked. 'It was marvellous what you did!' Then she turned to Mr Barber. 'Poor girl. I think she's a bit shocked. She must lie down and then go home. She's been a very, very brave girl.'

So Lucy went home, pale and subdued. When Mum and Dad heard the story they realised at once how the fire had started. They didn't say anything then because Lucy was so obviously upset. Besides, what could they say?

Lucy didn't know what to do next. Her new power was so uncontrollable, and much as she disliked Maureen Best, Lucy didn't want to make anybody go up in smoke, and that was what she was afraid would happen next, unless she learned how to control herself.

6

A Testing Time

For several days after the fire at school Lucy was quiet and moody. Both Mum and Dad tried to cheer her up, but with no success.

'I think she's scared,' said Mr King. 'I think she's discovered she has this extraordinary power and it frightens her. We ought to do something to try and help her.'

Mrs King laughed nervously. 'Perhaps we could strap a fire-extinguisher to her back?' she suggested.

'Not a bad idea,' laughed Mr King. 'Or maybe we should give her a water-pistol to carry round. No – I was wondering about taking her to see Dr Evans, or to the hospital and get some tests done.'

'What's the point? There's nothing wrong with her, Harold. The only problem is that she can fly, levitate anything she likes and make things burst into flames. That's normal – for Lucy.'

There didn't seem to be anything they could do. Then, one afternoon, Mr King was reading the newspaper when he came across an article that interested him. He mentioned it to his wife.

'There's a piece here about a Research Centre that's investigating para-psychology – you know, the strange things that some people are able to do, like bending spoons by stroking them or making things happen just by thinking about them.'

'Do they investigate people who can fly through the air?' asked Mrs King, half jokingly.

'That's just it. Why shouldn't they be able to help with Lucy? Perhaps they can find out how she makes things explode?'

'I suppose it's worth a try if it will help Lucy,' Mrs King said slowly. 'Give them a ring in the morning.'

The Research Centre were very interested when they heard about Lightning Lucy, and they asked Mr King to bring her along as soon as possible. Mr King took a day off work and drove Lucy to the Centre, an old rambling house set in huge grounds.

'I wouldn't mind living here,' Dad said to Lucy as they drove up the drive.

'It's too big,' said Lucy. 'And I bet it's got ghosts.'

'You're not scared of ghosts, are you?'

'No, of course not!' lied Lucy. 'But I expect Nicholas is.'

They were greeted at the Centre by a large, breathless man wearing thick spectacles that made his eyes seem twice as large as normal. 'Hallo, hallo!' he boomed. 'I'm Professor Brownsmith-Jones and you must be Lucy. Hallo Lucy! I'm Professor Brownsmith. bother, I've told you that already, haven't I? No point in telling you again, is there?

Well, come in, come in, come in. Don't stand on the doorstep like um, like people er standing on the doorstep. Ha ha! Silly me!' The professor showed them into his study, still chuckling away to himself. He sat them down on chairs and seated himself behind his desk in a huge leather swivel chair.

'Well!' he cried. 'I hear you can do all sorts of special things Lucy. Perhaps you'd show me, eh?'

Lucy looked blankly at Dad. 'What shall I do?' she whispered. Mr King smiled encouragingly. 'Why don't you fly round the room a little?'

It seemed a strange thing to ask and Lucy felt rather silly flying slowly round the room with nothing to do. Whenever she had flown before it was for a special purpose. She slipped back to her chair and sat down, whilst the faint red glow slowly faded from her body.

Professor Brownsmith-Jones had risen from his chair and he stood in the middle of the room with his eyes almost popping out from the sides of his spectacles.

'Did I see what I think I saw?' he demanded.

'Yes,' said Mr King rather proudly.

The professor began to walk quickly in tight circles, round and round, talking all the time. 'This is quite, quite extraordinary. Quite amazing! A girl who can fly, and why can a girl fly? I don't know. Does anybody know? I should think not, and why don't they know? Because they've never asked. What haven't they asked? I don't know, because I've forgotten what I'm talking about and I'm feeling rather dizzy so I'd better sit down. Where is everything?'

He stood still and waited for the room to stop swimming round him. Then he stared across at Lucy. 'And what else can you do?' he demanded.

'I can make things float,' said Lucy.

'Make things float?' The professor looked a trifle disappointed. 'Like boats?'

'No. Float in the air.'

'Oh! You mean like planes?' suggested the professor.

'You'd better show him,' murmured Dad. So Lucy got up and pointed at the professor and before he could say 'help!' he found himself rising into the air.

'Help!' he squeaked, when he overcame his own surprise. 'Put me down, please,' I can't stand heights!'

Lucy gently allowed the professor to land on the carpet. He got out a large handkerchief and mopped his sweating brow.

'I mean float like that,' explained Lucy.

'It's quite amazing,' gabbled the professor. 'Most unusual. I must do some tests at once and find out where your power is coming from.' He squinted at Lucy suspiciously.

'You haven't got special batteries hidden in your socks, have you?'

Lucy spluttered at the very idea, and shook her head. Mr King grinned quietly to himself, and the professor sighed.

'Well, you must come through into the laboratory and I'll connect you up to my new multi-positronic electro-defeebilizer.'

Lucy looked anxiously back at her father. He smiled and winked at her. 'You'll be alright,' he said. 'I won't be far away.' Lucy bit her lip and trailed after the professor.

The laboratory was enormous. It ticked and clicked and hummed with a hundred different gadgets. Rows of TV monitors along one wall displayed heart beats, pulse rates and brainwaves. In one corner a large computer chattered away to itself.

But what Lucy noticed most of all was the massive chair in the centre of the room. It was like a dentist's chair, only wider and longer. Wires sprouted from all over it and trailed away to mysterious boxes. Little lights flashed on and off. The professor hurried round switching things on and tapping dials. He pointed at the couch.

'You hop up there and I'll get you connected up. Now why won't the anti-static googlebender come on. You're a silly thing, aren't you? Yes, you are!'

While the professor talked to his instruments, Lucy climbed onto the couch and lay back. She gazed up at the ceiling and saw, for the first time, a weird machine hanging there. It glittered with reflected light, and looked like nothing so much as an alien space-ship. Lucy shivered.

'Ah! Good girl,' cried the professor. 'Now, I'll pop the electro-defeebilizer on.' He flicked a switch and the machine slowly descended, humming quietly to itself. It hovered above Lucy's curls. She squeezed herself down into the couch, away from the glistening metal gadget.

'No need to worry,' said the professor cheerfully. 'It's quite harmless. See, I'm wearing it myself.' He fitted the headpiece over his own bald dome, gave a little jump and a squeak, and whipped the headpiece off quickly. 'Ooh! Just a tiny shock! Nothing to worry about!'

Lucy smiled to herself. Electric shocks were one thing that she *was* used to. After all, she'd had lightning go right through her. The professor dropped the headpiece over her and she felt a warm tingle. Lucy settled back and relaxed.

Professor Brownsmith-Jones fastened something round her wrists. 'These bands will record your pulse,' he explained. He fastened a wider band across her stomach. 'This one will tell me what you had for breakfast. Ha ha ha! Silly me, just a joke. Comfortable? Yes, yes. Don't run away now, and off we go.'

He danced from one instrument to the next, flicking switches. The room vibrated with the steady hum of electricity, and dials began to twitter away. Little lights blinked on and off. Spurts of paper came from the computer.

'Fantastic, fantastic!' cried the professor, looking from one thing to the next. 'It's all working. My goodness, yes. I can see from your pulse rate you're still alive. That's a good thing. Let's see what happens when we switch on the multi-positronic electro-defeebilizer!

He plugged a fistful of coloured wires into Lucy's headpiece and immediately Lucy felt very weird. It was the strangest feeling she had ever experienced, as if all the inside parts of her body were rushing upwards, leaving her skin to struggle after it, longing to catch up.

Her head swam, and it seemed that her brain was filled with tiny dots of light, flashing on and off. It was altogether horrible and made her feel ill. Lucy wanted to stop. She tried to open her mouth to call out, but her lips wouldn't move and her tongue felt huge and useless. Her whole body felt huge and useless and the lights inside her head flashed ever brighter and faster, like warning signals spelling out danger.

Lucy screwed up her eyes and desperately tried to concentrate her thoughts on the defeebilizer, certain that it was the cause of her nightmare. Her brain was filled with a whirring noise that steadily grew louder. The couch started to tremble and its castors jiggled on the floor. A red haze surrounded the whole unit and tiny sparks began to dart from Lucy's fingers and hair.

A deep, low hum rumbled throughout the lab and Lucy's couch lifted from the ground and rose towards the ceiling, slowly swinging round as it did so. Brownsmith-Jones gave a startled cry and leaped towards it.

'Come back! Come down!' he yelled, and grabbed hold of the passing foot rest. It didn't do him any good. The professor left the ground for the second time that morning. He clung frantically to the bottom of the couch and closed his eyes.

The whole laboratory was now filled with the rising drone of over charged electricity. Machines began to rattle and bounce on their shelves and Lucy crackled all over and thin whip-lashes of sparks leaped from her body.

The TV monitors began to rise into the air. Everything in the lab began to take off, lifting up to the ceiling and trailing wires behind like a hundred kite strings. The smaller instruments flew up from their shelves and whizzed across the room from side to side. Tweezers clattered against the window. Scissors clanged against cupboards and some of the sharper tools flung themselves at the walls and ceiling and stuck there, quivering.

Meanwhile the computer was churning out paper messages faster and faster and the entire floor was now covered with a thick carpet of computer print-out. Stuck up high against the ceiling, Professor Brownsmith-Jones screamed for assistance. 'Help!!'

Mr King burst into the lab, crunching across a sea of paper. He twisted and ducked as instruments whistled past his head, threatening to slice his ears and nose off.

'Switch everything off!' pleaded the professor from on high.

Mr King raced round the room flicking and unplugging. The hum subsided. The machines slowly descended and piled themselves up on the shelves and floor. The great couch landed safely and Professor Brownsmith-Jones slumped to the floor, groaning. Lucy's eyelids flickered. Dad bent over her anxiously.

'Are you all right?' he asked. Lucy opened her eyes and smiled up at him. She gave a long sigh.

'It started off horrid,' she said. 'But then it got better and better. I had a lovely dream. I dreamt the whole world was taking off.'

'You weren't far wrong,' said Dad. Then Lucy saw all the paper and mess and the professor still groaning on the floor.

'Is Mr Brownblackgreen all right?' she asked.

'Brownsmith-Jones,' mumbled the professor. 'Brownsmith-Jones, Brownsmith-Jones. I think I'm dead. Can you take my pulse for me? I'm sure I'm dead and this must be Hell. Oh dear, oh dear.'

Mr King and Lucy helped the professor to get up and tidy the lab. The poor professor had to admit that there was nothing he could do to help. His instruments had been unable to record Lucy's powers at all. She was simply too strong for them.

'I could hardly believe it,' the professor exclaimed as he said goodbye to them. 'Everything just went out of control.'

'Yes,' said Mr King, shaking the professor's hand. 'Lucy does have that effect on things rather.' Hearing this, Lucy went quiet. She began to wish that just for once she could do something helpful.

7

Lucy gives the Piano a Lesson

Lucy and Nicholas were not looking forward to moving for two reasons. First of all they hated the idea of leaving the old house. It was like being told to throw out a favourite jumper. The second reason was that their moving day fell on the same day as the Grand Summer Fair, which took place in the park. They would miss everything.

Mr King tried to cheer them up. 'You'll soon get used to the new house, and we might get some peace and quiet there too, if Lucy doesn't do anything too spectacular for a while.' He wrapped some plates and packed them into a big wooden crate.

Lucy and Nicholas were soon involved in packing their own bedrooms. Everything had to go into boxes, and by the time moving day came, almost the whole house had been shoved into packing cases and stacked downstairs, ready to go. Only the beds had to be dismantled and the carpets rolled up.

'Do remember that the removal men are going to be working very hard,' said Mrs King. 'Don't get in their way.'

'Can't we help at all?' asked Lucy.

'Yes, you can help at the other end by unpacking your boxes and putting your clothes away neatly.'

'Oh that will be great fun!' groaned Lucy. 'Won't that be exciting, Nicky?'

Mrs King turned on her daughter. 'Don't call him Nicky!'

'But really I prefer being called Nicky,' admitted Nicholas.

'Oh for goodness' sake! Don't you start too. As if we haven't got enough to think about today. Now please keep out of the way.'

'But I could be really useful,' Lucy protested. 'I could make things float into the new house, and the removal men wouldn't have to do anything at all.'

But Mrs King went on shaking her head. 'Definitely not. I don't think I could cope with flying wardrobes and supersonic armchairs today. Please keep out of it.'

Mr King came in and told Lucy and Nicholas to go and play for a while, while they got the van loaded. Reluctantly the two children went off, with much grumbling and groaning.

It took ages to load the van. Lucy and Nicholas watched from an upstairs window as the removal men went backwards and forwards carrying load after load. Into the van went cupboards and chairs and boxes and carpets and the TV and the fridge and the new cooker – everything. There was only one thing left.

Lucy hoped they would leave the piano behind, but no, there it went, rumbling down the path like some strange, stiff dinosaur. The van had an air-operated tail gate, so once the piano was on the gate it was hoisted to the same height as the van. All the men had to do was push it inside.

Lucy wrinkled up her nose in disgust and went downstairs. The house looked odd now that it was empty. It didn't feel like their house at all.

'We're ready to go,' called Mum. They piled into the car and set off in front of the van. Half way there the car broke down.

'What a wonderful start,' shouted Dad, kicking a front tyre angrily. The removal van had to tow them the rest of the way.

The new house was almost at the top of a steep hill. At the bottom was the town centre, and at the top a rambling park where the Grand Summer Fair was always held. When the van pulled up outside the new house, the road was already full of excited people. Some were hurrying down to see the big band parade and watch all the floats go by. Others were struggling up the hill, to get to the park and join in the fun. Nobody wanted to miss anything.

'Just our luck,' groaned Lucy. 'We'll miss everything.'

But Mr King had other ideas. He put one hand in his trouser pocket. 'Lucy, Nicholas! I think the best thing for you to do is go off and enjoy the fair while Mum and I sort things out. I'll give you a pound each, all right? Don't spend it all at once.'

Dad fished two one pound notes from his pocket and handed them over. Nicholas danced round and round shouting with delight, but Lucy carefully held her money up to the light and peered hard at it.

'Is it real?' she asked. 'Is it a genuine pound note?'

Dad gave her a playful punch. 'Cheeky devil! Go and enjoy yourselves. But don't get into any trouble!' He watched them set off down the hill. Mrs King came over and slipped one arm through his. 'That was a good idea,' she said. 'Now perhaps we shall be able to unpack in peace.'

It didn't take long for Lucy and Nicholas to quarrel over what they would do first. Nicholas wanted to go straight to the park and Lucy wanted to see the floats. But when Lucy told Nicholas there'd be a Formula 1 racing car in the procession, he agreed to go down to the High Street.

'How do you know it's going to be there?' asked Nicholas.

'Robert told me. He knows Gary Burnett and Gary's dad owns the big garage near the school. I think the racing car has something to do with him because I saw a photo, and there's "Burnett's Garage" written all down both sides.'

Nicholas frowned. 'What? Why does Mr Burnett want writing down his sides?'

'Not Mr Burnett's sides, you dope,' groaned Lucy. 'Down the sides of the racing car. It's for advertising.'

When they reached the bottom of the hill the
parade had already started. Round the corner it
came, with the band in the lead and the floats
behind. The brass instruments shone in the sun.
The trumpets blared and the drums boomed.
Everybody shouted and cheered and waved. Lucy
and Nicholas soon got caught up with watching
everything, and quite forgot that they were in the
middle of moving house.

Near the top of the hill the house moving was going quite well, with Nicholas and Lucy safely out of the way. The last thing to be moved was the piano. The removal men got it down from the van all right, but they had great difficulty getting it up the kerb, which was very high. There were only two men and the piano was extremely heavy.

'Hang on,' said one. 'I'll come to your end and give a hand.' Then as soon as he let go of his end the piano began to roll sideways down the hill.

'Grab it quick!' yelled the second man, and he threw himself after the piano, but his weight only helped shove the piano faster on its way. The great instrument slipped from his grasp and trundled away down the hill, rapidly gaining speed.

Cars coming up the hill suddenly found themselves trying to dodge a rumbling, roaring monster charging down the hill in great zig-zags. The cars screeched and swerved, hooters honking, and there were several near misses as the piano raced past.

A crowd of people came chasing pell-mell after the runaway, shouting advice above the thundering echoes of the piano strings and the zinging of the little metal castors on the road.

'Stop that piano!'

'Call the police!'

'Watch out!'

Nobody at the bottom of the hill could hear them because of the parade. The band went trumpeting round the corner and up the hill, and down the hill came the speeding piano, intent upon joining them. The band went wild, scattering in all directions as the piano cut a path straight through their midst. Trumpets and drums were left in the middle of the road. The music became a series of shrill squeaks, and the crowd joined in with their shouts of panic.

With all that noise going on it was little wonder that Lucy thought something had gone wrong. She ran to the corner and looked around. There was chaos everywhere, with frightened bandsmen shinning up lamp-posts and women snatching their children to safety as the piano thundered past them down the hill.

Without thinking twice Lucy was up in the air and swooping low across the panicking crowds, leaving a long trail of glorious sparks behind. She zoomed up behind the piano and pointed her outstretched arms at it. A stream of glittering red came from her fingertips, gathering round the rattling monster. Lucy concentrated her mind, intent upon slowing the death-trap down. From the corner of her eye Lucy became aware of people and shops and cars, all rushing into view.

In a moment she knew that she couldn't slow the piano down in time. It was certain to crash, with terrifying results. She summoned up all her power and glared furiously at the instrument.

The lid flew off. The sides blew apart. Smoke poured from the top and in a flash of gold it burst into flames and collapsed on the spot, just a few metres from the racing car, whose driver had leaped out and was trying to hide under a giant tuba.

Somebody ran forward with a fire extinguisher and sprayed the smoking remains of the piano. Lucy landed on the pavement and wiped her brow. It had been a close thing. Instantly she was surrounded by people, yet she felt strangely awkward. It was bound to lead to more attention and that was just what Mum and Dad didn't want. As soon as she could she gave everybody the slip, found Nicholas and went quietly home.

Mr and Mrs King were sitting in the front room, surrounded by unpacked boxes, listening to Nicholas telling them all that had happened.

'Why does it always happen to you?' asked Mrs King, when he'd finished. Lucy was silent. 'That was our best piano too. Now you've got nothing to practice on.'

They were interrupted by a knock at the door. Standing outside was Mr Burnett. 'I've just popped up from the garage to say thank you. That was incredible Lucy! I could hardly believe my eyes. I was sure that piano was going to smash my racing car to pulp. I could see thousands of pounds vanishing in front of my eyes. Then you swooped down and Wham! Amazing! I'm very, grateful.'

Mr Burnett sat down and talked for a while. Lucy went upstairs. She wanted to be by herself. She lay on her bed and stared gloomily at the ceiling. She heard the front door bang.

'Lucy!' Dad was calling from the bottom of the stairs. 'Lucy, come down!' Mum and Dad and Nicholas were waiting in the front room. They were all grinning like monkeys.

'I don't know how you do it,' said Mr King. 'Mr Burnett was so pleased by the way you saved his racing car that he's going to get rid of our old car for us and give us a new one to replace it. Well, almost new anyway. How about that!'

Lucy gasped. 'What? A new car? Really? Really and truly?'

'Really and truly,' laughed Mum.

'Yippee!' cried Lucy. Perhaps life wasn't so bad after all. They were getting a new car and she wouldn't have to do piano practice any more because she'd just blown the piano up.

'And I had another brainwave,' said Dad, smiling. 'Our old piano was insured. All we have to do is put in a claim and we can get a new piano for Lucy to practice on. After all, it's only fair. If she can get me a new car, the least I can do is get her a new piano.'

'Aren't you lucky,' teased Mum.

Lucy let out a long groan and pretended to faint.